CONTENTS

Introduction
Chapter 1. The AI Revolution and Your Financial Future ... 1
Chapter 2: Understanding AI Without the Jargon ... 5
Chapter 3: Finding Profitable Opportunities with AI ... 12
Chapter 4: Building Your First AI-Enhanced Business ... 15
Chapter 5: Creating Passive Income Streams with AI ... 18
Chapter 6: Automating Your Business with AI for Maximum Efficiency ... 21
Chapter 7: Leveraging AI for Advanced Marketing Strategies ... 29
Chapter 8: Enhancing Customer Experience with AI ... 37
Chapter 9: AI in Sales: Boosting Conversions and Maximizing Revenue ... 46
Chapter 10: Building an AI-Driven Culture: Empowering Your Team for Success ... 55
CONCLUSION. ... 62
Acknowledgement ... 65

INTRODUCTION

Welcome To The Age Of Ai-Powered Benefits

The world is changing faster than ever before. As artificial intelligence (AI) reshapes industries, disrupts traditional business models, and fuels innovation, one truth has become undeniable: the businesses that embrace AI today will be the ones leading tomorrow. From small startups to global corporations, AI is no longer just a tool for the tech-savvy elite—it's a game-changer accessible to anyone willing to adapt, innovate, and seize its potential.

Welcome to "AI-Powered Profits," your guide to unlocking the transformative power of AI to elevate your business, outpace your competition, and create lasting value. Whether you're an entrepreneur, a business leader, or a curious professional, this book will equip you with the knowledge and strategies needed to harness AI in practical, profitable ways.

Why AI, and Why Now?

AI has moved from the realm of science fiction to the heart of everyday business operations. Today, AI powers recommendation systems on your favorite shopping platforms, personalizes your entertainment choices, and enables businesses to anticipate customer needs before they even arise. What once seemed like futuristic technology is now a tangible force driving productivity, efficiency, and growth.

Businesses that leverage AI effectively are already reaping the rewards. They're cutting costs with automation, making smarter decisions with data-driven insights, and delivering personalized experiences that keep customers coming back. But AI isn't just about big corporations; it's also about leveling the playing field, enabling small businesses and entrepreneurs to compete in ways they never could before.

This book is your roadmap to tapping into that power. Whether you want to streamline operations, supercharge your marketing efforts, or revolutionize how you serve customers, AI-Powered Profits will show you how to do it—ethically, strategically, and effectively.

What You'll Discover in This Book?

This isn't a book filled with technical jargon or complex theories. It's a practical guide designed for action-takers who want to see real results. Here's what you can expect:

Clarity on AI Basics: If AI feels overwhelming or overly technical, don't worry. We'll break it down into simple concepts that anyone can understand.
Proven Strategies for Success: Learn how businesses across industries are using AI to solve problems, create efficiencies, and drive growth—and how you can replicate their success.
Tools You Can Use Today: From AI-powered chatbots to advanced analytics platforms, we'll explore tools you can start

implementing immediately, no matter your budget or experience. Future-Proofing Your Business: As AI continues to evolve, so too must your strategies. We'll discuss how to stay agile, adapt to new technologies, and maintain your competitive edge.

Why This Book Matters Now?

We're at a pivotal moment in history. AI is no longer a competitive advantage; it's becoming a necessity for survival in an increasingly digital economy. The businesses that act now to embrace AI will thrive, while those that hesitate risk falling behind.

But adopting AI isn't just about tools or technology—it's about mindset. It's about creating a culture of innovation, empowering your team, and aligning your vision with the limitless potential of AI. This book isn't just about making your business better today; it's about building a foundation for sustained growth and success in the years to come.

Your Journey Starts Here

This book is your call to action. Whether you're a seasoned entrepreneur, a corporate executive, or someone just beginning to explore the world of AI, AI-Powered Profits is designed to inspire, educate, and empower you.

By the time you finish this book, you'll have the confidence, knowledge, and tools to transform your business using AI. You'll understand what's possible, how to make it happen, and why taking action today is the key to securing a brighter, more profitable tomorrow.

The future isn't coming—it's already here. The question is, are you ready to take advantage of it?

Let's get started. The age of AI-Powered Profits begins now.

CHAPTER 1. THE AI REVOLUTION AND YOUR FINANCIAL FUTURE

We are living through one of the most transformative periods in human history. Artificial intelligence (AI), once a concept confined to science fiction, is now a powerful force driving innovation across every industry. From automating tedious tasks to making complex predictions, AI is reshaping the way we live, work, and most importantly, make money.

In this chapter, we'll explore why the AI revolution is an unparalleled opportunity for individuals like you to create wealth. You'll learn how AI is leveling the playing field, empowering anyone with a vision to seize the moment and thrive in a rapidly changing world.

What is the AI Revolution?

The AI revolution refers to the widespread adoption of intelligent systems capable of performing tasks that once required human intelligence. These systems can analyze vast amounts of data, recognize patterns, and make decisions faster and more accurately than humans ever could.

Consider this: AI can now create artwork, compose music, write articles, and even help doctors diagnose diseases. What does this mean for you? It means the tools that were once reserved for tech giants and researchers are now available to entrepreneurs, freelancers, and everyday people looking to innovate and earn.

Why Now is the Time to Act?

Timing is everything when it comes to opportunity, and the AI revolution is no exception. Here's why now is the perfect time to embrace AI:

Accessibility: AI tools and platforms have become incredibly user-friendly. You no longer need to be a programmer to harness the power of AI. Platforms like ChatGPT, MidJourney, and Jasper allow users to create content, design visuals, and even build apps with minimal effort.

Cost-Effectiveness: What used to require expensive hardware and software is now affordable—or even free. Many AI tools offer entry-level plans that anyone can use to get started.

Demand for Innovation: Businesses and consumers are hungry for AI-driven solutions. Whether it's streamlining processes, improving customer experience, or creating new products, the appetite for innovation is insatiable.

Exponential Growth: AI technology is advancing at an unprecedented rate. This creates an ongoing stream of new opportunities to exploit, ensuring you can stay ahead of the curve if you remain informed and adaptive.

The Financial Impact of AI

AI isn't just a tech trend—it's an economic game-changer. According to studies, AI is expected to contribute over $15 trillion to the global economy by 2030. But here's the kicker: much of that wealth will be created by individuals and small businesses that recognize and act on AI's potential.

Let's look at some examples:

1. E-commerce: AI is revolutionizing online shopping by offering personalized product recommendations and automating customer service through chatbots. Small businesses using these tools can compete with much larger players.

2. Freelancing: AI-powered tools like Canva, Grammarly, and coding assistants are helping freelancers deliver high-quality work faster, allowing them to take on more clients and increase earnings.

3. Content Creation: AI is enabling creators to write books, produce videos, and design logos at a fraction of the traditional cost, opening the door to new income streams.

The key takeaway? AI is an equalizer. It gives you access to tools and capabilities that can dramatically increase your earning potential, regardless of your background or technical expertise.

Mindset for Success in the AI Era

To capitalize on the AI revolution, you need to adopt the right mindset. Here's what it takes:

Curiosity: Stay eager to learn and explore. The AI space is evolving rapidly, and keeping up with the latest trends will position you for success.

Adaptability: Don't fear change—embrace it. Be ready to pivot your strategies as new AI tools and opportunities emerge.

Action-Oriented Thinking: AI rewards those who take initiative. Don't wait for the perfect moment or tool; start experimenting and iterating now.

Value Creation: Focus on how you can use AI to solve problems for others. Whether you're improving efficiency, creating better experiences, or saving time, adding value will always lead to profit.

A Glimpse of What's Ahead

This book is your roadmap to thriving in the AI-driven economy. In the chapters to come, you'll learn how to identify opportunities, harness AI tools, and build systems that generate income while you sleep.

AI is here, and it's reshaping the world faster than ever before. The question is not whether you'll be affected by the AI revolution but whether you'll use it to your advantage.

The time to act is now. Let's start building your AI-powered future.

Ready to dive deeper? In Chapter 2, we'll break down AI into simple, actionable concepts so you can begin your journey without feeling overwhelmed. Let's get started!

CHAPTER 2: UNDERSTANDING AI WITHOUT THE JARGON

Artificial intelligence (AI) can seem like a mysterious and complex field, but it doesn't have to be. In this chapter, we'll break down the key concepts behind AI into simple, actionable ideas that anyone can understand. By the end of this chapter, you'll have a clear grasp of what AI is, how it works, and most importantly, how you can use it to make money.

What is AI?

At its core, artificial intelligence is the simulation of human intelligence in machines. It's about creating systems that can learn, reason, and make decisions just like a human—or in some cases, even better. But let's make this simpler:

AI is a tool that helps you solve problems, save time, and achieve things faster. It's like having an assistant who never gets tired, works 24/7, and constantly gets smarter the more you use it.

How Does AI Work?

To understand AI, you don't need to dive into coding or algorithms. Here's a high-level explanation:

Data is the Fuel:

AI systems learn by analyzing data. This could be anything from customer feedback to social media posts or even images. The more data AI has, the better it performs.

Learning from Patterns:

AI identifies patterns in the data. For example, an AI tool might notice that customers who buy a certain product are also likely to buy another product. This is how AI systems make predictions.

Improvement Over Time:

AI uses a process called "machine learning" to improve. This means it gets better the more it's used, adapting to new information and refining its output.

Types of AI You'll Encounter

AI comes in various forms, but here are the types you'll most likely use in your money-making ventures:

1. Natural Language Processing (NLP):

AI that understands and generates human language. Tools like ChatGPT can help you write articles, craft emails, or even draft entire books.

2. Computer Vision:

AI that interprets visual data like images or videos. Applications include creating designs, enhancing photos, or automating visual inspections in e-commerce.

3. Predictive Analytics:

AI that forecasts future trends based on historical data. This is invaluable for stock trading, customer behavior analysis, or market research.

4. Automation Tools:

AI that handles repetitive tasks, such as scheduling social media posts, responding to customer inquiries, or sorting emails.

Why AI is Not as Complicated as It Seems

Many people hesitate to dive into AI because it seems intimidating. But here's the truth: you don't need a degree in computer science to use AI effectively. Today's AI tools are designed to be user-friendly, often requiring nothing more than basic computer skills.

Think of AI as a smartphone app. You don't need to know how the app was built to use it. Similarly, you don't need to understand the deep technical details of AI to leverage its capabilities.

Common AI Tools and How They Work

Here are some popular AI tools and how you can use them to make money:

1. ChatGPT (by OpenAI):

What It Does: Generates human-like text based on your input.

How to Use It: Write blog posts, create marketing content, or draft product descriptions in minutes.

Monetization Ideas: Freelance writing, content creation, or social media management.

2. Canva (with AI integrations):

What It Does: Simplifies graphic design with AI-powered suggestions and templates.

How to Use It: Design logos, social media posts, or marketing materials.

Monetization Ideas: Start a design service or sell pre-made templates.

3. Jasper AI:

What It Does: Helps create long-form content like articles, emails, and ad copy.

How to Use It: Automate content creation for businesses.

Monetization Ideas: Offer copywriting services or content strategy consulting.

4. MidJourney or DALL·E:

What It Does: Creates stunning images and artwork from text descriptions.

How to Use It: Generate unique designs for your projects.

Monetization Ideas: Sell custom art, design merchandise, or offer creative services.

Real-Life Examples of AI in Action

To make AI less abstract, let's look at real-world scenarios where people have used AI to create profitable ventures:

5. Freelance Writing:

A writer used AI to increase productivity, completing 10 articles per day instead of 3. This allowed them to take on more clients and triple their income.

6. E-commerce Success:

An online store owner used AI to analyze customer behavior and suggest products. Sales increased by 30% within three months.

7. Social Media Growth:

A marketer used AI tools to schedule posts, analyze performance, and even generate captions. This freed up time to focus on strategy, leading to better client retention.

The AI Learning Curve

Getting started with AI might feel overwhelming, but here's how to ease into it:

1. Start Small:

Pick one AI tool and master it. For example, use ChatGPT to automate your email writing before exploring other applications.

2. Experiment:

Try different tools and see which ones align with your goals. Many AI platforms offer free trials, so you can explore without a financial commitment.

3. Learn as You Go:

Don't aim for perfection right away. AI tools are designed to be intuitive, and you'll get better with practice.

How to Identify the Best AI Tools for Your Needs?

With so many AI tools available, choosing the right one can be daunting. Here's a step-by-step approach:

1. Define Your Goals:

What do you want to achieve? Whether it's saving time, making money, or enhancing creativity, your goal will guide your choice of tools.

2. Research and Reviews:

Look for reviews and case studies to see how others have used the tool. Platforms like YouTube and blogs often have tutorials.

3. Test the Tool:

Most AI tools offer free trials or demo versions. Use these to get a feel for the platform before committing.

4. Assess the Learning Curve:

Some tools are more beginner-friendly than others. Choose one that matches your skill level.

Overcoming Common AI Misconceptions

Let's debunk some myths about AI:

Myth: AI will replace humans.
Reality: AI enhances human capabilities. It's a tool, not a replacement.

Myth: AI is only for tech-savvy people.
Reality: Modern AI tools are designed to be accessible to everyone.

Myth: AI is too expensive.
Reality: Many AI tools are affordable or even free for basic use.

Preparing for the AI-Powered Economy

Understanding AI is not just about learning new tools—it's about adopting a mindset that embraces innovation and adaptability. The world is moving fast, and those who are willing to learn and experiment will reap the rewards.

In the next chapter, we'll dive deeper into identifying profitable opportunities with AI. Whether you're looking to start a new venture, grow your existing business, or create passive income streams, you'll discover actionable strategies to turn AI into your biggest financial asset.

Let's get ready to explore how you can transform ideas into income with the power of AI!

CHAPTER 3: FINDING PROFITABLE OPPORTUNITIES WITH AI

One of the most exciting aspects of AI is its ability to open up new, profitable opportunities that were once unimaginable. In this chapter, we'll explore how to identify these opportunities, so you can turn AI into your ultimate wealth-building tool.

The Power of AI to Spot Trends

AI excels at analyzing vast amounts of data and recognizing patterns. This is a powerful tool when it comes to identifying business trends, market needs, and emerging opportunities. The key to making money with AI is using it to uncover opportunities that others may not see. Here's how you can leverage AI for this:

Predictive Analytics

AI tools like machine learning algorithms can predict future trends based on historical data. For instance, AI in finance can predict stock price trends, while in retail, it can predict which products will be popular next season. By leveraging predictive analytics, you can get ahead of the curve and tap into profitable markets before they become saturated.

Sentiment Analysis

AI tools can monitor social media, blogs, and forums to gauge public sentiment around a specific product, service, or idea. Using sentiment analysis, you can uncover trending topics or products that are gaining traction. Imagine being able to predict the next viral product or the next big business niche—AI can help you do just that.

Customer Behavior Insights

AI can track customer behavior on websites, mobile apps, and e-commerce platforms. This information helps you understand what customers are looking for, what they value, and what they are most likely to purchase. AI tools like Google Analytics and customer relationship management (CRM) software can reveal trends that can inform new product ideas or services that meet customer demand.

Monetizing AI-Driven Market Insights

AI isn't just about predicting trends or analyzing data; it can also directly lead to profits. Here's how you can monetize market insights:

Create and Sell Data-Driven Reports

Use AI to analyze a specific industry or market, then package your insights into a report that businesses or investors can purchase. For example, if AI analysis reveals an underserved market or a gap in consumer demand, you can sell that information to entrepreneurs looking to capitalize on new opportunities.

Develop AI-Powered Products

Use insights gathered from AI-driven research to develop new products or services that fill gaps in the market. Whether it's a mobile app, a consumer product, or a SaaS solution, AI can guide you toward what customers are actually looking for.

AI in Affiliate Marketing and E-Commerce

If you're interested in e-commerce or affiliate marketing, AI can be your secret weapon to optimize your business for maximum profit. Here's how:

1. Automated Ad Campaigns

AI tools like Google Ads, Facebook Ads, and Instagram Ads now use machine learning to automatically optimize your ad campaigns. They adjust your bidding strategy in real-time based on which ads are performing best, helping you maximize your return on investment (ROI) with minimal effort.

2. Personalized Shopping Experiences

AI can be used to create a hyper-personalized shopping experience for customers. By analyzing browsing history and purchase behavior, AI can recommend products customers are more likely to buy. E-commerce businesses that use AI-driven recommendations often see an increase in conversion rates and customer retention.

3. AI-Powered Dropshipping

Dropshipping businesses are notorious for their low profit margins, but AI can change the game by automating many of the time-consuming tasks involved. AI can help you manage inventory, choose trending products to sell, and even optimize product descriptions and pricing strategies. With the right tools, AI can make dropshipping a much more profitable venture.

CHAPTER 4: BUILDING YOUR FIRST AI-ENHANCED BUSINESS

Now that you understand how to identify profitable opportunities, it's time to dive into how to build an AI-powered business from the ground up. In this chapter, we'll discuss everything from idea generation to automation, and show you how to use AI to grow your business.

Step 1: Find Your Niche

The first step in building any business is choosing the right niche. AI can help you with this by providing insights into what markets are trending and where there is unmet demand. You can leverage AI tools like Google Trends, BuzzSumo, and industry reports to identify profitable niches in real time.

Step 2: Automate Your Business Operations

One of the most powerful ways AI can benefit your business is through automation. By automating repetitive tasks, you can focus more on strategy and growth. Here are some key areas where AI can automate your business:

Customer Service Automation

AI-powered chatbots can handle customer service inquiries, provide support, and even complete transactions without any human intervention. Popular platforms like Intercom, Drift, and Zendesk use AI to handle customer interactions, saving you time and money.

Marketing Automation

Tools like Mailchimp, HubSpot, and ActiveCampaign use AI to optimize your email marketing campaigns, segment your audience, and personalize messages. These platforms can even automatically generate email subject lines, content, and offers based on customer preferences and behavior.

Inventory and Supply Chain Management

AI tools can predict stock demand, automate inventory management, and streamline your supply chain. This reduces costs, minimizes overstocking or stockouts, and allows you to run a more efficient business.

Step 3: Monetizing Your AI-Enhanced Business

Once you have automated the key components of your business, it's time to start generating revenue. AI can enhance your monetization strategy in several ways:

Subscription Models

With AI, you can offer personalized subscription services. For example, an AI-powered e-learning platform can tailor courses to individual students based on their progress and preferences. Subscription models can be highly profitable, providing consistent and predictable revenue streams.

Productized Services

AI can help you turn your expertise or services into automated products that customers can purchase. For example, if you're a graphic designer, AI-powered design tools can allow you to create customizable templates that customers can buy and use themselves. This creates passive income with minimal effort.

Step 4: Scale Your Business with AI

Once your business is running smoothly, it's time to scale. AI can help you achieve scalability in a variety of ways:

Data-Driven Decisions

Use AI tools like Google Analytics, Tableau, and Power BI to analyze your business performance. AI can provide insights into which products or services are performing best and help you focus on scaling those areas.

Personalization at Scale

AI allows you to personalize customer experiences at scale. For example, you can use AI-powered email marketing platforms to send tailored messages to thousands of customers without manual intervention. Personalization boosts customer engagement, loyalty, and sales.

CHAPTER 5: CREATING PASSIVE INCOME STREAMS WITH AI

One of the most powerful ways to use AI is to build passive income streams that continue to generate money with minimal active involvement. In this chapter, we'll explore different ways you can use AI to create automated income that works for you around the clock.

1. AI-Driven Content Creation

Content creation is one of the best ways to generate passive income, and AI can help you scale your efforts quickly. With AI tools like ChatGPT, you can write blog posts, create video scripts, and even generate social media posts in a fraction of the time it would take manually.

Blogging for Passive Income

With AI, you can create content that attracts organic traffic to your blog. Use SEO optimization tools powered by AI to rank higher in search engines and drive traffic to your site. You can then monetize this traffic through affiliate marketing, sponsored posts, or selling your own products.

YouTube Automation

AI can help you generate scripts and video titles that attract views. AI tools can also help with editing and optimizing your videos for SEO, allowing you to publish content regularly without spending too much time on the technical aspects.

2. AI in Affiliate Marketing

Affiliate marketing is a great way to earn passive income, and AI tools can help you optimize your strategy. AI can help you choose the best products to promote, track your performance, and analyze which affiliate programs are performing the best.

Automating Product Recommendations

Use AI to automatically recommend products to your audience based on their interests and behavior. Personalized recommendations increase conversion rates and boost your affiliate earnings.

Optimizing Campaigns

AI can also automate your ad campaigns, targeting the right audience with the most relevant offers. This increases your chances of earning commissions without having to manually monitor campaigns.

3. AI for Investment Strategies

AI can be used to automate investment strategies, creating another form of passive income. Many investors are turning to AI-powered tools that help them choose stocks, bonds, and other investments based on data-driven algorithms.

Robo-Advisors

Platforms like Betterment and Wealthfront use AI to manage investments. By using these services, you can create a diversified portfolio that grows over time, generating passive returns with minimal intervention.

Cryptocurrency Trading

AI tools can help you automate cryptocurrency trading by using algorithms to buy and sell based on market trends. Tools like Cryptohopper and 3Commas use AI to make trading decisions automatically, helping you earn passive income from crypto investments.

CHAPTER 6: AUTOMATING YOUR BUSINESS WITH AI FOR MAXIMUM EFFICIENCY

In today's fast-paced world, efficiency is everything. Business owners and entrepreneurs are always on the lookout for ways to work smarter, not harder. AI, in its various forms, provides the ultimate solution to automation, allowing businesses to operate more efficiently, reduce human error, and save time—ultimately leading to higher profits. In this chapter, we'll dive deep into how you can use AI to automate business processes, enhance productivity, and scale your operations for long-term success.

Understanding the Power of Automation

To understand how AI-driven automation can revolutionize your business, it's essential to first grasp the concept of automation. At its core, automation involves using technology to complete tasks that would otherwise require human intervention. This can range from basic, repetitive tasks like scheduling to more complex processes like predictive analytics or customer support.

While traditional automation was limited to physical tasks (think industrial robots), AI-powered automation has expanded into intellectual tasks as well. This means AI can now manage workflows, make decisions, optimize resources, and even engage with customers—all without human oversight. For example, imagine a business that needs to process thousands of customer inquiries every day. AI-powered chatbots can handle this task, providing personalized responses based on user input, all while operating 24/7.

The key advantage of automation is that it frees up your time and energy for more strategic, revenue-generating activities, allowing you to scale without significantly increasing costs. And with AI, the potential for automation is virtually limitless.

Key Areas of Your Business You Can Automate with AI

Let's take a closer look at the key areas in your business where AI automation can make the biggest impact:

Customer Support Automation

Providing excellent customer support is crucial to retaining clients and ensuring long-term success. But managing customer inquiries can be time-consuming and labor-intensive. Here's where AI shines. With AI-powered chatbots and virtual assistants, you can automate customer service operations, offering immediate responses to common queries and issues.

AI Tools to Consider: ChatGPT (for customer queries), Zendesk (for automating ticket management), Drift (for real-time customer conversations).

How It Works: Once a customer reaches out with a question, the AI chatbot can quickly analyze the inquiry and provide an accurate, personalized response. In more complex cases, AI can escalate the issue to a human agent, while still offering suggestions or context to assist the agent.

Benefit: Customer satisfaction increases because customers get fast, efficient service. You'll also save time and money by reducing the need for a large customer service team.

Email Marketing Automation

Email marketing is one of the most effective ways to nurture leads and maintain relationships with customers, but manually crafting and sending emails can be time-consuming. AI-powered email automation tools can segment your audience, create personalized email content, and send emails at the optimal time for each recipient.

AI Tools to Consider: Mailchimp, ActiveCampaign, HubSpot (email automation and segmentation tools).

How It Works: AI can analyze customer behavior, such as which emails they open, which links they click, and when they interact with emails. With this information, the system can automatically create personalized email campaigns tailored to the recipient's preferences, making your outreach more effective.

Benefit: Increased email open rates, higher engagement, and improved conversion rates without the need to manually manage campaigns.

Content Creation and Curation

Content creation is another area where AI can save you an enormous amount of time. Whether you're writing blog posts, creating social media content, or drafting newsletters, AI tools can help you produce high-quality content in a fraction of the time it would take manually.

AI Tools to Consider: Jasper AI, Copy.ai, Writesonic (for generating written content), Canva (for creating visual content).

How It Works: These AI tools use natural language processing (NLP) algorithms to understand the topic at hand and generate relevant, high-quality content. For example, you can input a few keywords or topics into Jasper AI, and it will generate an entire blog post for you. Similarly, Canva's AI can generate stunning designs based on your brief, even suggesting color schemes and fonts.

Benefit: You can rapidly scale your content marketing efforts, consistently publishing high-quality material without the need for hiring additional writers or designers.

Sales and Lead Generation Automation

AI can significantly improve your sales process by automating lead generation, qualification, and nurturing. AI tools can help you identify high-potential leads, personalize outreach efforts, and even close deals automatically using chatbots or AI-powered sales assistants.

AI Tools to Consider: Salesforce Einstein, HubSpot Sales, LeadSquared.

How It Works: AI algorithms analyze data from various sources—social media, customer interactions, previous purchases—to predict which leads are most likely to convert. AI can then follow up with personalized emails, schedule meetings, and even offer product recommendations based on the lead's interests.

Benefit: This reduces the workload for your sales team, improves conversion rates, and helps you focus on the leads that matter most.

Social Media Management

Social media is a crucial aspect of modern business, but manually posting content, responding to comments, and analyzing engagement can take up a lot of time. AI can streamline these processes, making social media marketing more efficient.

AI Tools to Consider: Hootsuite, Buffer, Sprout Social (for scheduling and engagement automation), SocialBee (for content curation and posting).

How It Works: AI tools can schedule posts across multiple platforms, analyze the best times to post, and even generate content ideas based on trending topics. Some platforms, like Hootsuite, allow AI to respond to messages or comments based on keywords, ensuring timely interactions.

Benefit: You'll increase your online presence without sacrificing valuable time, allowing you to maintain a consistent, professional social media presence across all channels.

Inventory and Supply Chain Automation

Managing inventory and supply chain logistics is a time-consuming process that can benefit greatly from AI. AI systems can predict demand, automatically reorder stock, and optimize supply chain routes to reduce costs and improve delivery times.

AI Tools to Consider: TradeGecko (inventory management), Llamasoft (supply chain optimization).

How It Works: By analyzing past sales data and seasonal trends, AI can predict which products are likely to sell in the coming weeks, helping you optimize your inventory levels. In supply chain management, AI can analyze factors like weather patterns, delivery times, and traffic data to suggest the most efficient delivery routes.

Benefit: You'll reduce stockouts, minimize overstocking, and streamline your supply chain processes, leading to lower operational costs and faster deliveries.

How to Implement AI Automation in Your Business?

Now that we understand the key areas where AI automation can be applied, let's discuss how to effectively implement AI into your business.

1. Start Small and Scale Gradually

If you're new to AI automation, start with one process that can benefit from automation. For example, if your business receives a high volume of customer inquiries, begin by implementing a chatbot. Once you're comfortable with that tool and see the benefits, consider expanding into other areas like email marketing or content creation.

2. Choose the Right Tools for Your Business

Not all AI tools are created equal, so it's essential to choose the ones that align with your business goals and budget. Look for tools that integrate with your existing systems (like CRM or email marketing platforms) and provide a user-friendly interface. Many AI platforms offer free trials or demos, so take advantage of these opportunities to test different solutions before making a commitment.

3. Monitor and Optimize Your AI Systems

Once you've implemented AI automation, it's essential to monitor its performance and make adjustments as needed. AI systems often improve over time, but it's important to track their effectiveness in real-time. Use data and analytics to measure how well the automation is performing and make adjustments to fine-tune the process.

4. Train Your Team

If you have a team, ensure that everyone is on board with the transition to AI automation. Train your team on how to use the new tools, and emphasize how automation will help them save time and increase productivity. Proper onboarding will lead to a smoother implementation and ensure that your team fully utilizes the potential of AI.

5. Ensure Data Privacy and Security

As you automate business processes, you'll be handling a significant amount of customer data. It's crucial to prioritize data privacy and security, especially if you're working with sensitive information. Use AI tools that comply with data protection regulations like GDPR and implement strong cybersecurity measures to safeguard your data.

6. Scaling Your Business with AI Automation

Once you've automated various processes in your business, it's time to scale. AI gives you the ability to grow your business without adding significant overhead. Here are a few strategies to help you scale with AI:

7. Replicate and Expand Successful Systems

After automating one aspect of your business, replicate that system in other areas. For example, if your email marketing campaigns are generating good results through automation, apply the same approach to other marketing channels, like social media or paid advertising.

As AI handles more tasks, your business will become more efficient. You'll be able to process orders faster, engage with more customers, and deliver products or services at a higher rate. Use this increased efficiency to expand your offerings and grow your customer base.

CHAPTER 7: LEVERAGING AI FOR ADVANCED MARKETING STRATEGIES

AI has revolutionized the marketing world. Gone are the days when businesses relied solely on traditional marketing methods, like television ads, cold calls, or door-to-door promotions. Today, the tools and techniques available through AI can enable businesses to reach their target audience in more personalized and scalable ways. In this chapter, we'll explore how you can leverage AI to optimize your marketing strategies, drive customer engagement, and maximize your return on investment (ROI).

The Role of AI in Modern Marketing

Artificial intelligence is transforming how businesses approach marketing. Whether it's through automated content creation, hyper-targeted advertising, customer segmentation, or predictive analytics, AI is reshaping the landscape. AI can gather and analyze enormous amounts of data faster and more accurately than humans ever could, enabling businesses to make data-driven decisions that enhance marketing outcomes.

By leveraging AI, businesses can:

Target the right audience: AI enables businesses to analyze customer data and segment audiences more effectively, ensuring they reach the most relevant groups.

Personalize the customer experience: AI tools help create personalized experiences, improving customer satisfaction and engagement.

Predict trends and customer behavior: AI-powered predictive analytics can forecast future trends, giving businesses a competitive edge in understanding and anticipating customer needs.

Automate marketing tasks: From content creation to social media management and customer support, AI tools can automate tedious tasks, freeing up marketers to focus on more strategic initiatives.

AI Tools and Techniques for Effective Marketing

To implement AI successfully in your marketing efforts, it's essential to understand the various AI tools and techniques that can be applied across different aspects of your marketing strategy. Let's break it down into key marketing components:

1. Customer Segmentation and Targeting

Effective marketing relies on targeting the right people at the right time. AI allows businesses to analyze vast amounts of customer data and automatically segment customers based on behavior, demographics, interests, and past interactions. This allows businesses to serve tailored messages to specific groups, ensuring they're engaging with the right audience in a personalized way.

How AI Enhances Segmentation:

Behavioral Targeting: AI tools analyze user behavior on websites, mobile apps, and social media to build customer profiles. These profiles help identify which types of products or services are most relevant to each individual.

Predictive Segmentation: By using machine learning, AI can predict which segments are most likely to convert into paying customers based on past data. This means you can focus your marketing efforts on the most valuable segments.

Dynamic Targeting: AI also enables real-time dynamic targeting, meaning you can modify and personalize ads or content based on the user's interaction with your website or platform at any given moment.

AI Tools for Segmentation and Targeting:

Google Analytics and HubSpot: These tools allow you to analyze customer data and generate reports that reveal key audience segments.

Salesforce Einstein: Salesforce's AI-powered tools help automate customer segmentation and predictive targeting for higher ROI on marketing campaigns.

Benefits of AI-Driven Segmentation:

Enhanced customer experience through personalized messaging

Improved conversion rates by focusing on high-value prospects

Higher marketing ROI through more effective targeting

2. Content Personalization

One of the most powerful applications of AI in marketing is content personalization. AI enables businesses to deliver highly personalized experiences to customers across various touchpoints, from email marketing campaigns to web pages, ads, and product recommendations.

How AI Personalizes Content:

Dynamic Content: AI algorithms can automatically adjust the content of emails, web pages, or ads based on a user's profile, behavior, or stage in the customer journey. For example, a returning customer might see product recommendations based on their past purchases, while a new visitor might be shown introductory content.

Email Campaigns: AI-powered tools like Mailchimp and ActiveCampaign use customer data to personalize email content, subject lines, and even send times based on user behavior.

Product Recommendations: On e-commerce sites, AI algorithms analyze browsing and purchasing history to recommend relevant products to customers, significantly increasing the chances of additional sales.

Chatbots and Virtual Assistants: AI-powered chatbots can engage customers directly, offering personalized recommendations and assisting with purchases based on previous interactions.

AI Tools for Personalization:

Dynamic Yield and Optimizely: These tools enable dynamic personalization across websites and emails based on user data and behavior.

Algolia and Recombee: These tools are used to enhance search functionality and provide product recommendations using AI-powered algorithms.

Benefits of Content Personalization:

1. Improved customer satisfaction through tailored experiences

2. Higher conversion rates by showing customers exactly what they want

3. Increased customer retention by creating more meaningful interactions

4. Predictive Analytics and Customer Insights

Understanding customer behavior and predicting future trends is crucial for optimizing marketing efforts. Predictive analytics, powered by AI, can analyze historical data and predict future actions, helping businesses stay ahead of the competition and make informed decisions.

How Predictive Analytics Works:

Customer Lifetime Value (CLV): AI algorithms can predict the lifetime value of each customer, helping businesses prioritize high-value customers and tailor retention strategies accordingly.

Churn Prediction: AI can predict when a customer is likely to churn (i.e., stop using your product or service), allowing businesses to intervene with targeted retention strategies.

Trend Forecasting: AI uses past consumer behavior data to identify trends, enabling businesses to adjust their marketing campaigns to align with emerging trends before they become mainstream.

AI Tools for Predictive Analytics:

Tableau and Power BI: These business intelligence platforms use AI to provide predictive analytics and data visualization, helping marketers make data-driven decisions.

Customer.ai: An AI-powered tool that predicts customer behavior based on past interactions, providing insights into future customer needs and actions.

Benefits of Predictive Analytics:

1. More accurate forecasting of sales and marketing performance
2. Data-driven decision-making that enhances campaign

effectiveness

3. Proactive marketing strategies that anticipate customer needs and reduce churn

4. Automating Campaign Management

AI-powered tools can help automate various aspects of campaign management, from optimizing ad spend to scheduling content. Automation not only saves time but also improves campaign performance by ensuring that your efforts are optimized for maximum impact.

How AI Automates Campaigns:

Ad Bidding Optimization: AI tools like Google Ads and Facebook Ads use machine learning to automatically adjust bidding strategies, ensuring that your ads are shown to the right people at the right price.

Campaign Optimization: AI can continuously monitor your marketing campaigns, adjusting messaging, targeting, and budget allocation based on performance in real-time. This helps ensure that every campaign is optimized for maximum efficiency and results.

Multichannel Management: AI tools allow you to manage marketing campaigns across multiple channels (e.g., email, social media, paid ads) from one platform, automating tasks like content scheduling, post publishing, and engagement tracking.

AI Tools for Campaign Automation:

1. Google Ads and Facebook Ads Manager: These platforms utilize AI to automate bidding and optimize ads in real time.

2. Hootsuite and Buffer: These tools allow for automation of social media content scheduling and engagement, leveraging AI to

suggest the best times to post.

Benefits of Campaign Automation:

1. Time-saving by automating repetitive tasks
2. Improved ROI through continuous campaign optimization
3, Enhanced marketing consistency across multiple channels
4. AI-Powered Social Media Marketing

Social media marketing has become an indispensable part of any business strategy. AI can help optimize social media campaigns by automating content scheduling, managing engagement, and identifying key influencers or trends. AI's ability to analyze social media data in real-time can help businesses respond quickly to customer feedback and adjust their strategy accordingly.

How AI Enhances Social Media Marketing:

Sentiment Analysis: AI tools can scan social media posts, reviews, and comments to gauge public sentiment around your brand. This can help you respond to negative feedback quickly and capitalize on positive interactions.

Content Curation: AI algorithms can suggest content topics based on trending keywords or your audience's interests. This ensures that you are always posting relevant, engaging content.

Influencer Marketing: AI can identify key influencers in your industry by analyzing social media data, helping you partner with individuals who have the most influence over your target audience.

AI Tools for Social Media Marketing:

Sprout Social and Hootsuite Insights: These tools provide real-time sentiment analysis and help you track brand mentions and engagement.

BuzzSumo: A content research tool that uses AI to identify trending topics, popular content, and influencers within your industry.

Benefits of Social Media AI:

1. Faster response times to customer feedback and inquiries

2. Better-targeted content that resonates with your audience

3. Increased engagement through smarter content and influencer partnerships

Conclusion: The Future of Marketing with AI

As we've explored throughout this chapter, AI offers businesses a myriad of opportunities to optimize and automate their marketing strategies. By leveraging AI for customer segmentation, content personalization, predictive analytics, campaign automation, and social media marketing, businesses can achieve a new level of efficiency, targeting, and customer engagement.

The future of marketing is undoubtedly AI-driven, and the companies that adopt these technologies today will be in the best position to thrive in the marketplace of tomorrow. As AI technology continues to evolve, its impact on marketing will only grow, creating even more opportunities for businesses

CHAPTER 8: ENHANCING CUSTOMER EXPERIENCE WITH AI

In an increasingly competitive marketplace, customer experience has become the key differentiator that can make or break a business. As customers demand more personalized, efficient, and seamless interactions with brands, businesses are turning to artificial intelligence (AI) to meet these expectations. AI has the potential to transform every aspect of the customer journey—from pre-purchase research to post-purchase support.

In this chapter, we'll explore how AI can enhance customer experience management by improving service delivery, personalizing interactions, and streamlining communication. By embracing AI-powered solutions, businesses can create exceptional customer experiences that drive loyalty, increase satisfaction, and ultimately, boost profitability.

The Importance of Customer Experience

Customer experience (CX) refers to the overall perception a customer has of a brand based on their interactions across all touchpoints, from browsing a website to speaking with customer service representatives. Today, providing a great customer experience is more important than ever. A study by Forrester revealed that 86% of customers are willing to pay more for a better customer experience, while 73% of consumers say that a positive experience is a key factor in influencing their brand loyalty.

As businesses face growing competition, standing out in a crowded marketplace requires not only offering quality products or services but also delivering a superior customer experience. AI, with its ability to analyze data, predict behavior, and automate interactions, is transforming how businesses engage with customers, making it easier to deliver consistent, personalized, and impactful experiences.

AI in Customer Service: Automation and Efficiency

AI-driven automation has become a game-changer in the world of customer service. Chatbots, virtual assistants, and AI-powered helpdesks are now commonplace, providing fast and efficient solutions to customers while significantly reducing the need for human intervention. Let's take a closer look at how AI is improving customer service operations.

AI Chatbots: The Future of Customer Support

One of the most widely adopted AI technologies in customer service is the chatbot. AI-powered chatbots can engage with customers in real time, answering questions, resolving issues, and guiding users through common processes, all without the need for a human representative. These bots use natural language processing (NLP) to understand and respond to customer inquiries in a conversational manner.

How Chatbots Enhance Customer Service:

24/7 Availability: Chatbots are always online, ensuring that customers can get support at any time, even outside of business hours.

Instant Responses: Chatbots provide immediate replies to

customer questions, drastically reducing response times and improving customer satisfaction.

Cost Efficiency: By handling common inquiries, chatbots reduce the need for a large customer service team, lowering operational costs.

Personalized Interactions: Modern chatbots can analyze customer data to provide tailored responses, making interactions feel more personalized.

AI Tools to Consider:

Intercom: A conversational AI platform that helps businesses automate customer support and engagement.

Drift: Another popular AI-powered tool that offers real-time chat functionality for sales and customer support.

Zendesk: Known for integrating AI-powered features like chatbots, self-service portals, and automated ticket routing to improve support efficiency.

Benefits of Chatbots:

1. Improved customer satisfaction through fast, accurate responses

2. Reduced customer service workload, freeing up human agents for more complex tasks

3. Cost savings and efficiency improvements in managing support requests

4. Virtual Assistants: Human-Like Customer Engagement

Virtual assistants, powered by AI, are another tool that businesses can use to enhance customer experience. These assistants go beyond simple chatbot capabilities by offering more advanced features, such as voice recognition, multilingual support, and complex task handling. Virtual assistants can answer questions, provide recommendations, schedule appointments, and even perform transactions—creating an experience that feels closer to speaking with a human representative.

How Virtual Assistants Improve Customer Experience:

Multichannel Support: Virtual assistants can operate across a wide range of channels, including websites, mobile apps, and social media platforms, allowing customers to interact with brands seamlessly.

Context-Aware Conversations: AI assistants can remember customer history, preferences, and prior interactions, offering contextually relevant support that feels personal and efficient.

Enhanced Self-Service: Virtual assistants empower customers to find solutions to their problems independently, reducing wait times and providing faster resolutions.

AI Tools to Consider:

1. Google Assistant and Amazon Alexa: Both of these virtual assistants are widely used to provide hands-free customer service experiences.

2. Ada: An AI-powered virtual assistant that integrates with existing platforms like websites, apps, and customer support systems to automate inquiries and responses.

3. LivePerson: A conversational AI platform that enables businesses to interact with customers across messaging channels like SMS, WhatsApp, and Facebook Messenger.

Benefits of Virtual Assistants:

1. Real-time, 24/7 customer engagement across multiple channels

2. Personalized, context-aware interactions that improve customer satisfaction

3. Increased efficiency in handling routine customer queries, allowing human agents to focus on more complex issues

Personalized Experiences: Tailoring Interactions with AI

Personalization is one of the most powerful tools businesses can use to build strong customer relationships and foster loyalty. AI makes it possible to deliver highly personalized experiences by analyzing customer data, behaviors, and preferences. Whether it's delivering targeted recommendations, customizing product offerings, or sending personalized communications, AI allows businesses to interact with customers in a way that feels relevant and unique to their needs.

Product Recommendations

Personalized product recommendations are a staple in modern e-commerce. AI systems can analyze a customer's browsing history, purchase behavior, and preferences to suggest relevant products. This helps businesses increase sales by encouraging customers to discover new items that align with their interests.

How AI Powers Product Recommendations:

1. Recommendation Algorithms: AI uses machine learning algorithms to analyze vast amounts of customer data and identify patterns in behavior, helping businesses recommend products

that are more likely to resonate with the individual.

2. Real-Time Suggestions: AI can offer real-time product suggestions during browsing or checkout, further enhancing the likelihood of additional sales.

AI Tools for Product Recommendations:

Recombee: An AI-powered recommendation engine that helps e-commerce platforms offer personalized suggestions to customers.

Algolia: A search and discovery API that personalizes product search and recommendations using AI-driven algorithms.

Benefits of Personalized Product Recommendations:

1. Increased average order value (AOV) by encouraging additional purchases

2. Higher conversion rates due to relevant suggestions based on past behaviors

3. Enhanced customer satisfaction and loyalty through tailored shopping experiences

Personalized Email Marketing

AI can also take personalization to the next level in email marketing. By analyzing customer data, AI tools can tailor subject lines, content, and offers to individual customers, ensuring that each email feels highly relevant to the recipient.

How AI Personalizes Email Marketing:

Dynamic Content: AI can customize the content of emails in real time, ensuring that each recipient sees offers or product suggestions tailored to their preferences.

Optimal Send Time: AI tools can analyze customer behavior and determine the best time to send emails to maximize open rates and engagement.

Segmentation and Targeting: AI automatically segments your audience based on behavior and demographic data, allowing businesses to send more targeted emails to the right people.

AI Tools for Personalized Email Marketing:

Mailchimp and ActiveCampaign: These platforms provide AI-powered automation features, such as personalized email content and optimized send times.

Persado: An AI tool that optimizes email subject lines and copy by analyzing customer preferences and emotional triggers.

Benefits of AI in Email Marketing:

Improved open rates and engagement through personalized content

Higher conversion rates with more relevant offers

Increased customer retention due to tailored communication

AI-Driven Insights and Analytics for Customer Experience

One of the most valuable applications of AI in customer experience is its ability to gather, process, and analyze large volumes of data to provide actionable insights. These insights help businesses better understand customer preferences, pain points, and behaviors, allowing them to make informed decisions that improve the overall experience.

Sentiment Analysis and Feedback Monitoring

AI-powered sentiment analysis tools can help businesses monitor customer sentiment across multiple platforms, including social media, review sites, and support channels. By analyzing text, AI can gauge whether customer feedback is positive, negative, or neutral, allowing businesses to respond quickly to issues or capitalize on positive feedback.

How Sentiment Analysis Works:

Natural Language Processing (NLP): NLP algorithms enable AI to analyze customer reviews, social media comments, and support conversations to identify sentiment and emotions.

Real-Time Feedback: AI can provide real-time insights into how customers are feeling about your brand, enabling businesses to address concerns before they escalate.

AI Tools for Sentiment Analysis:

MonkeyLearn and Lexalytics: These AI tools provide sentiment analysis by processing large amounts of customer feedback, social media posts, and reviews.

Brandwatch: A social listening tool that uses AI to track customer sentiment across online channels and provide real-time insights.

Benefits of Sentiment Analysis:

1. Proactive management of customer concerns and issues

2. Improved brand reputation by addressing negative sentiment quickly

3. Enhanced customer satisfaction through timely and relevant

responses

4. AI and Customer Experience: The Future

As AI technology continues to evolve, its impact on customer experience will only grow. The future of customer service lies in the combination of automation and personalization. As AI becomes more sophisticated, businesses will be able to provide more human-like interactions while maintaining the efficiency and scalability that automation provides. By leveraging AI, businesses can not only meet but exceed customer expectations, leading to increased loyalty, satisfaction, and profitability.

Key Takeaways:

AI is transforming customer service by automating tasks, enhancing personalization, and providing real-time insights.

Chatbots, virtual assistants, and AI-driven recommendations can improve the speed, accuracy, and relevance of customer interactions.

Personalization through AI helps businesses create tailored experiences, leading to higher customer satisfaction and increased sales.

Sentiment analysis and predictive analytics allow businesses to proactively manage customer relationships and improve brand perception.

As AI continues to advance, the future of customer experience will be shaped by the ability of businesses to leverage these technologies to provide innovative, efficient, and personalized services. The businesses that embrace AI today will be well-positioned to lead the charge in delivering exceptional customer experiences in the years to come.

CHAPTER 9: AI IN SALES: BOOSTING CONVERSIONS AND MAXIMIZING REVENUE

Sales is the lifeblood of any business. Every company, regardless of its size or industry, aims to close more deals, increase revenue, and build a loyal customer base. In today's highly competitive and data-driven marketplace, artificial intelligence (AI) is emerging as a powerful tool for sales teams, helping them increase conversions, streamline processes, and personalize interactions.

By automating time-consuming tasks, analyzing vast amounts of data, and providing valuable insights, AI enables sales teams to focus on high-impact activities that drive results. In this chapter, we'll dive deep into how AI can revolutionize your sales efforts —from lead generation to sales forecasting and everything in between. We'll also explore the tools and strategies you can use to harness AI for maximizing your sales performance.

The Changing Landscape of Sales

In the past, sales were largely driven by manual processes, relying on personal relationships, intuition, and traditional outreach methods like cold calling, emailing, and in-person meetings. However, the rise of digital technologies and the availability of vast amounts of customer data have fundamentally changed the way sales teams approach their work.

Today, sales professionals are expected to manage complex customer journeys, which often involve multiple touchpoints across various channels. Customers are more informed, and they expect personalized, relevant interactions with businesses at every stage of their buying process. For sales teams to stay competitive, they need to adopt new technologies that enable them to be more efficient, data-driven, and customer-centric.

Artificial intelligence offers precisely the tools and capabilities needed to meet these new demands. AI's ability to analyze massive datasets, predict customer behavior, and automate routine tasks enables sales teams to be more focused and effective. By leveraging AI, businesses can deliver highly personalized sales experiences that improve conversion rates, increase revenue, and build long-lasting customer relationships.

AI-Powered Lead Generation: Identifying High-Quality Prospects

Generating leads is one of the most crucial tasks for any sales team. However, finding qualified leads can be a time-consuming and challenging process. AI is transforming how businesses approach lead generation by automating the identification of high-quality prospects and helping sales teams prioritize their efforts.

AI in Lead Scoring

Lead scoring is a method of ranking prospects based on their likelihood of converting into paying customers. Traditionally, lead scoring involved manual processes, where salespeople would assess leads based on criteria like demographics, job titles, and past interactions. AI, however, can automate this process by analyzing vast amounts of data and identifying patterns that indicate a lead's likelihood of conversion.

How AI Enhances Lead Scoring:

Data-Driven Insights: AI algorithms analyze customer data, including website activity, social media interactions, and past purchases, to generate more accurate lead scores.

Predictive Analytics: AI uses historical data to predict which leads are most likely to engage with your business and make a purchase, allowing sales teams to focus on high-potential opportunities.

Dynamic Lead Scoring: As a lead interacts with your brand, AI can dynamically adjust their lead score based on new data, ensuring that sales teams are always working with the most up-to-date information.

AI Tools for Lead Scoring:

HubSpot Sales Hub: A popular sales automation tool that includes AI-powered lead scoring features to help prioritize prospects.

Salesforce Einstein: Salesforce's AI platform, which can predict and score leads based on customer behavior and engagement data.

Infer: An AI-driven lead scoring platform that uses machine learning to predict which leads are most likely to convert into sales.

Benefits of AI in Lead Scoring:

1. More accurate identification of high-value leads
2. Increased sales efficiency by focusing resources on the most promising prospects
3. Better alignment between sales and marketing teams through shared data-driven insights

AI for Lead Qualification

Lead qualification refers to the process of determining whether a lead is a good fit for your business. AI can automate much of this process by analyzing leads' behaviors, demographic information, and past interactions to determine whether they are ready for a sales conversation.

How AI Optimizes Lead Qualification:

Behavioral Analysis: AI can track a lead's behavior across various touchpoints, such as email opens, website visits, and product inquiries, to assess their level of interest and engagement.

Personalized Outreach: Based on the insights gathered from AI, sales teams can send highly personalized messages to leads, offering the right product recommendations or solutions based on the lead's interests and needs.

Automated Qualification: AI can automate the qualification process by triggering follow-up actions or nudging sales reps to take specific actions based on lead activity.

AI Tools for Lead Qualification:

Outreach: This platform offers AI-powered lead qualification and engagement tools that help sales reps prioritize leads and automate outreach.

Conversica: An AI assistant that automatically engages and qualifies leads through email conversations, saving sales teams time and resources.

InsideSales.com: Uses AI to analyze lead data and provide insights into the best time to contact leads and how to approach them.

Benefits of AI in Lead Qualification:

1. Faster lead qualification with less manual effort

2. Higher-quality leads that are more likely to convert

3. Increased sales productivity as AI automates routine tasks and prioritizes the most promising leads

4. Driven Sales Outreach: Automating the Sales Process

Once a lead is qualified, the next step is outreach—engaging with the prospect and moving them down the sales funnel. AI can significantly improve this phase by automating outreach tasks, personalizing communication, and providing valuable insights into the most effective strategies.

Automating Email Campaigns

Email is one of the most effective ways to engage with prospects, but manually crafting and sending personalized emails to every lead can be time-consuming. AI-powered email automation tools can help sales teams create tailored emails, send them at optimal times, and analyze the performance of each campaign.

How AI Enhances Email Outreach:

Personalized Email Content: AI tools can generate personalized email subject lines, content, and product recommendations based on the recipient's behavior and preferences.

Optimal Send Time: AI algorithms analyze data to determine the best time to send an email, increasing the likelihood of it being opened and acted upon.

A/B Testing: AI tools can automatically test different email subject lines, content, and formats to determine which approach drives the most engagement and conversions.

AI Tools for Email Outreach:

Mailchimp and ActiveCampaign: These tools use AI to personalize email campaigns, optimize send times, and analyze campaign performance.

Reply.io: An AI-powered tool that automates email outreach and follow-ups, helping sales teams scale their efforts.

Benefits of AI in Email Outreach:

1. Increased open and response rates through personalized and timely emails
2. Improved sales conversion rates as emails become more relevant to leads
3. Better use of sales teams' time by automating repetitive tasks

AI for Sales Call Automation

While email and messaging are essential components of sales outreach, phone calls remain a critical part of the sales process. AI can assist in this area through tools that automate certain aspects of sales calls, such as lead qualification, information gathering, and follow-up scheduling.

How AI Automates Sales Calls:

Voice Recognition: AI tools like Google Assistant or Salesforce Einstein Voice can automatically transcribe calls and provide real-time insights to sales reps during conversations.

Call Scheduling and Follow-Up: AI can automatically schedule calls with leads based on their availability and ensure that follow-up calls are made at the right time.

Real-Time Call Insights: AI can analyze the tone and sentiment of customer conversations to provide sales reps with key insights about the lead's intent and interest.

AI Tools for Sales Call Automation:

Gong.io: Uses AI to analyze sales calls, providing sales teams with insights into conversation quality, sentiment, and key takeaways.

Chorus.ai: An AI-powered conversation analytics platform that records and analyzes sales calls to help sales reps improve their pitch and understand customer concerns.

Benefits of AI in Sales Calls:

Improved call efficiency with AI-generated insights and recommendations

Better customer engagement with data-driven approaches

Increased conversion rates by ensuring timely follow-ups and relevant conversations

AI for Sales Forecasting and Pipeline Management

Accurate sales forecasting is essential for effective business planning. AI can help sales teams make more accurate predictions about revenue, deal closure rates, and sales pipeline health by analyzing historical data and identifying patterns that humans might miss.

AI in Sales Forecasting

Traditional sales forecasting relies heavily on the experience and intuition of sales managers. However, AI can take this process to the next level by providing more precise and data-driven predictions.

How AI Improves Sales Forecasting?

Historical Data Analysis: AI analyzes historical sales data to identify trends, seasonality, and key factors that influence sales performance.

Predictive Modeling: Using machine learning algorithms, AI predicts future sales outcomes based on current pipeline data, enabling businesses to adjust strategies accordingly.

Scenario Planning: AI can model different scenarios and predict how changes in pricing, marketing efforts, or other factors will impact sales performance.

AI Tools for Sales Forecasting:

Clari: An AI-driven sales forecasting tool that uses real-time pipeline data to predict future sales and provide insights for decision-making.

Zoho CRM: Includes AI-powered forecasting capabilities that help sales teams predict revenue and optimize pipeline management.

Benefits of AI in Sales Forecasting:

1. More accurate predictions of revenue and sales outcomes
2. Better resource allocation based on predicted sales volume
3. Improved business decision-making through data-driven insights

Maximizing Revenue with AI

AI empowers sales teams to close deals faster, engage more effectively with prospects, and make better decisions based on real-time insights. By automating repetitive tasks, personalizing outreach, and analyzing sales data, businesses can increase their conversion rates, streamline their sales process, and maximize their revenue potential.

Key Takeaways:

AI can revolutionize lead generation, scoring, and qualification by automating manual processes and using data-driven insights to identify high-quality prospects.

AI tools help personalize outreach, optimize sales calls and emails, and automate follow-up, saving time and increasing conversion rates.

Sales forecasting becomes more accurate with AI, enabling businesses to plan and allocate resources more effectively.

By leveraging AI throughout the sales cycle, businesses can boost efficiency, improve their customer interactions, and ultimately, drive more revenue.

As the technology continues to evolve, the potential for AI to transform sales operations will only grow. The future of sales is increasingly reliant on AI-driven tools and strategies, and businesses that embrace these innovations will have a competitive edge in the market.

CHAPTER 10: BUILDING AN AI-DRIVEN CULTURE: EMPOWERING YOUR TEAM FOR SUCCESS

The integration of artificial intelligence (AI) into business operations is no longer a futuristic concept—it's happening right now. While adopting AI technologies is essential for staying competitive, it's equally important to build an AI-driven culture within your organization. An AI-driven culture goes beyond simply using AI tools; it's about empowering your team, fostering innovation, and aligning the entire organization around a common goal of utilizing AI to drive growth and profitability.

In this chapter, we'll explore how to create an AI-driven culture, from leadership buy-in to employee training, and how this cultural shift can set the foundation for long-term success. We'll dive into the steps you need to take to ensure your organization embraces AI and maximizes its potential to create value for both your business and your customers.

Why an AI-Driven Culture Matters?

AI is not just a tool for automating processes or analyzing data—it has the potential to fundamentally change how a business operates. However, to fully realize the benefits of AI, organizations need to cultivate a culture that embraces these transformative technologies. Without the right mindset and cultural alignment, the implementation of AI can be met with resistance, confusion, or even failure.

An AI-driven culture offers several benefits:

1. Increased Innovation: Employees are more likely to innovate when they are encouraged to leverage AI tools and technologies that enable them to work smarter and more efficiently.

2. Improved Decision-Making: AI can provide real-time insights that empower employees to make data-driven decisions with greater confidence.

3. Operational Efficiency: AI-driven automation reduces the time spent on manual tasks, enabling employees to focus on higher-value activities that contribute to the business's bottom line.

4. Enhanced Customer Experience: AI allows businesses to provide personalized, proactive services that meet the needs of customers more effectively and efficiently.

For AI to have a meaningful impact on your business, your company must foster a culture of openness, collaboration, and continuous learning. The leadership team must be actively involved in driving this cultural shift, ensuring that AI adoption is not just a top-down directive but a company-wide initiative that empowers employees at all levels.

Step 1: Leadership Buy-In and Vision

The first step in building an AI-driven culture is ensuring that leadership is fully committed to AI adoption. This commitment must go beyond just approving the purchase of AI tools or technologies; it must involve creating a vision for how AI can transform the business and investing in the resources necessary to make that vision a reality.

1. Define a Clear AI Vision: Leadership should articulate a clear

vision for how AI will be used across the organization. This vision should outline the objectives of AI adoption, whether it's improving operational efficiency, enhancing customer experience, or driving revenue growth. By defining a clear vision, leaders provide the direction and purpose for AI initiatives, making it easier for employees to understand why AI is important and how it will benefit them.

2. Invest in AI Resources: AI adoption requires both financial and human resources. Leaders should allocate the necessary budget for AI tools, platforms, and infrastructure. Additionally, companies must invest in the right talent, including AI specialists, data scientists, and IT support, to ensure that AI projects are executed effectively. For AI to succeed, it requires continuous investment in technology, training, and expertise.

3. Lead by Example: For AI adoption to take hold across an organization, leaders must demonstrate their commitment by using AI themselves. When leaders show that they're open to adopting new technologies, employees are more likely to follow suit. Whether it's using AI tools for decision-making, automation, or data analysis, leaders must be visible champions of AI adoption.

Step 2: Foster Cross-Department Collaboration

AI is not confined to any one department or function within a business. From marketing and sales to operations and finance, AI can be applied across the entire organization. As such, fostering cross-department collaboration is essential to building an AI-driven culture.

1. Break Down Silos: In many organizations, departments work in isolation, each with its own goals, metrics, and priorities. However, AI initiatives benefit from a more collaborative approach. By encouraging departments to work together on AI

projects, organizations can ensure that AI is applied to its full potential across various functions. For example, marketing teams can collaborate with data scientists to improve lead generation, while operations teams can work with AI experts to automate supply chain management.

2. Establish Cross-Functional AI Teams: Building cross-functional teams that include employees from various departments—data scientists, engineers, marketers, and other stakeholders—helps foster a collaborative environment where AI knowledge is shared, and business objectives are aligned. These teams can work on AI projects from ideation to implementation, ensuring that AI tools and technologies are deployed in ways that address the unique needs of each department.

3. Create a Shared Knowledge Base: Knowledge sharing is critical to the success of AI initiatives. Organizations should create platforms for employees to share their experiences with AI tools, discuss best practices, and collaborate on solving challenges. This can include regular AI workshops, webinars, or internal knowledge-sharing platforms where employees can exchange ideas and learn from one another.

Step 3: Empower Employees with AI Training and Education

1. One of the key challenges to building an AI-driven culture is overcoming the fear or uncertainty that often accompanies new technologies. Employees may feel that AI will replace their jobs or that they don't have the skills to leverage AI effectively. Providing the right training and education is crucial to dispelling these concerns and empowering employees to embrace AI.

2. Offer AI Training Programs: Employees should be given access to AI training programs that help them understand the basics of AI, its capabilities, and its potential applications in their daily

work. This could include online courses, workshops, and seminars on AI and machine learning. These programs should be designed for employees at all levels, from beginners to advanced users, and should focus on practical, hands-on learning.

3. Encourage Continuous Learning: AI is a rapidly evolving field, and to stay competitive, employees must be encouraged to keep learning. Offering ongoing training opportunities, such as access to the latest AI tools, resources, and certifications, will help employees stay up to date on the latest advancements in AI technology and learn how to apply them in their roles.

4. Provide Support and Resources: It's important to offer employees the support they need to succeed in an AI-driven environment. This includes providing access to AI experts who can offer guidance and troubleshooting support. Additionally, companies can create internal resources like AI FAQs, tutorial videos, and dedicated channels for AI-related questions to ensure that employees have the tools they need to use AI effectively.

Step 4: Encourage Innovation and Experimentation

An AI-driven culture thrives on innovation. Encouraging employees to experiment with AI tools and technologies and take calculated risks is essential for fostering creativity and finding new ways to leverage AI to improve business processes.

Promote a Growth Mindset: A growth mindset encourages employees to view challenges and setbacks as opportunities for learning and growth. In the context of AI, this means encouraging employees to experiment with new AI tools, test hypotheses, and explore innovative ways to apply AI to their work. Leaders should celebrate success but also embrace failure as part of the learning process, helping employees to feel more comfortable trying new ideas without fear of failure.

Create Innovation Hubs: Companies can establish innovation hubs or labs where employees can collaborate on AI projects, share ideas, and test out new concepts in a low-risk environment. These innovation hubs can serve as incubators for new AI-driven solutions and allow employees to work on projects that might not fit into the traditional workflow but have the potential to drive significant business value.

Reward Innovation: To motivate employees to push the boundaries of AI adoption, companies should reward innovation. This could be in the form of recognition, promotions, or even financial incentives for employees who come up with creative AI-driven solutions that positively impact the business. Recognizing and celebrating employees who embrace AI and innovate with it will encourage others to do the same.

Step 5: Measure and Optimize AI Performance

Once AI tools and technologies have been integrated into your business operations, it's important to measure their performance and continuously optimize their impact. Data-driven decisions should be made to ensure that AI is delivering the expected results and that any areas for improvement are identified and addressed.

1. Define Key Performance Indicators (KPIs): To measure the success of AI initiatives, businesses must define clear KPIs that align with their overall goals. These KPIs could include metrics like cost savings, productivity improvements, customer satisfaction scores, or revenue growth. By tracking these metrics, businesses can assess the effectiveness of their AI efforts and determine whether they're meeting their objectives.

2. Conduct Regular AI Audits: Regular audits of AI tools and processes can help identify inefficiencies, biases, or areas where

improvements can be made. Auditing your AI systems ensures that they continue to operate in line with business goals and that they remain ethical and unbiased in their decision-making.

3. Optimize AI Models: AI is not a "set it and forget it" technology. AI models must be continuously optimized and trained on new data to improve accuracy and relevance. As your business grows and changes, your AI systems should evolve to reflect new customer behaviors, market conditions, and technological advancements.

However, the true power of AI isn't just in the technology itself—it's in how you, as a business leader, choose to leverage it. Building an AI-driven culture is the foundation upon which success is built. By ensuring that leadership is aligned, employees are trained, and departments collaborate, you set the stage for a future in which AI becomes an integral part of your organization's DNA. As we've discussed in the final chapter, creating a culture that embraces innovation and continuous learning is crucial for maximizing the long-term value of AI.

CONCLUSION.

Harnessing AI for Unmatched Profitability and Growth

As we wrap up this journey through the landscape of AI-Powered Profits, it's clear that artificial intelligence isn't just a fleeting trend—it's a powerful and transformative force that has the potential to reshape every facet of business. From automating routine tasks and enhancing decision-making to revolutionizing customer experiences and driving revenue growth, AI offers a wealth of opportunities for businesses willing to embrace it.

Throughout this book, we've explored how AI can be integrated into key business functions—from sales and marketing to customer service and operations. We've examined the tools, strategies, and best practices that can help businesses unlock the true potential of AI to boost efficiency, optimize resources, and improve outcomes. Whether you're a small startup or a large corporation, AI can be a game-changer, provided you approach it strategically and with the right mindset.

The Road Ahead: Adapting to an AI-Driven Future

The future of business is increasingly defined by data, automation, and intelligence. AI is at the center of this transformation, and the sooner businesses adopt AI-driven strategies, the more competitive advantage they'll gain in the marketplace. As technology continues to advance at a rapid pace, the organizations that thrive will be the ones that are agile, innovative, and proactive in integrating AI across their operations.

As you reflect on the insights shared in this book, consider how AI can transform your own business. Look at your current processes—where are the bottlenecks? Where can automation drive efficiency? How can AI enhance the customer journey or provide deeper insights into your market? Whether through predictive analytics, intelligent automation, or personalized customer interactions, AI offers boundless possibilities for driving growth and achieving profitability.

But remember, adopting AI is a journey, not a destination. As you begin integrating AI into your business, be prepared to experiment, learn from failures, and iterate. AI will evolve, and so too must your strategies. The key is to remain flexible, continuously optimizing and refining your use of AI tools to stay ahead of the curve.

Take Action Today

If there's one key takeaway from this book, it's that now is the time to act. AI is no longer a luxury reserved for large enterprises or tech giants—it's accessible, scalable, and impactful for businesses of all sizes. The sooner you embrace AI, the sooner you'll begin reaping the rewards of increased efficiency, greater innovation, and higher profitability.

Start small if necessary—experiment with AI tools, explore use cases, and begin integrating AI into your workflows. From there, you can scale and expand, turning AI from a tool into a transformative business asset. Whether you're focusing on optimizing your sales pipeline, automating customer service, or improving supply chain management, there are countless ways to leverage AI to drive your business forward.

Remember, AI isn't just about replacing human effort; it's about enhancing it. By freeing up time and resources, AI allows your team to focus on higher-value tasks, innovate, and make smarter decisions. The future is bright for businesses that recognize AI's potential and adapt to this new technological landscape.

In closing, AI-Powered Profits isn't just a guide to using AI to enhance business operations—it's a blueprint for creating a future where AI is fully integrated into every aspect of your business. By building an AI-driven culture, empowering your team, and staying ahead of the curve, you'll set your business on the path to long-term growth, profitability, and success.

So, take the first step today—embrace AI, and unlock the doors to a world of new possibilities. The future is here, and it's powered by AI.

Your AI-powered journey begins now.

ACKNOWLEDGEMENT

1. Canva - For Design of the Cover
2. ChatGPT = For Content generation and idea creation

www.ingramcontent.com/pod-product-compliance
Lightning Source LLC
Chambersburg PA
CBHW071424220526
45469CB00004B/1429